K

The Birth of Flight:
A History of the Wright Brothers
Just for Kids!

BOOKCAPS

KidCaps is An Imprint of
BookCaps™
www.bookcaps.com

Table of Contents

About KidCaps

KidCaps is an imprint of BookCaps™ that is just for kids! Each month BookCaps will be releasing several books in this exciting imprint. Visit are website or like us on Facebook to see more!

The famous first flight of Orville Wright was in 1903.[1]

---

[1]   Image   source: http://www.wright-house.com/wright-brothers/Wrights.html

Introduction

The breeze was blowing steadily into Orville Wright's face as he walked around his and his brother's creation. It was a beautiful day here on the North Carolina beach, but both men were too preoccupied with what they were doing to notice it. Walking around the plane that they had built with their own hands, using their own design, the men checked the bolts, the wires, and the seat that the pilot would be sitting on. The breeze was constant and was about the right speed for the test. Everything was ready.

Orville and his brother Wilbur looked at each other and discussed who should be the pilot during this historic test flight. Deciding to flip a coin instead of wasting precious time debating, it was decided that Orville should be the pilot. Neither man argued; they both just got on with their respective jobs. Three lifeguards working on the beach had come over to help them and to watch their attempt and see what happened. They helped Orville and Wilbur position the plane at the start of the long sixty foot track that was laid out on the flat ground before them.

Orville climbed up into the plane and strapped himself into the seat. He checked to make sure that the seat could slide back and forth on its rails, as they had designed it to do, and that the wings flexed each time he did it. Check. He looked back over his shoulder to make sure that the tail moved when the wings did. Check. Finally, he waited while his brother got the two propellers spinning on the back of the aircraft.

Orville loved it when the engine was started, and the propellers started to spin. The plane felt less like something that they had built in their shop and more like a racehorse that was eager to start running. The plane came to life and the engine to his right started rumbling. He could feel the small plane pushing forward, trying to move, but blocks kept it from going down the track until his brother removed them. Wilbur checked the motion of the propellers, and everything looked good. The two brothers gave each other thumbs-up, and the blocks were released. Holding onto the wings to balance it as it raced down the railing, Wilbur ran alongside the plane as it gained speed.

The first feeling was always exciting, like riding a bicycle quickly down a hill. Orville's stomach felt like it had butterflies inside, and although he knew this was a serious moment during a serious experiment. He felt a little smile creep across his face. The plane rolled down the track, gathering the speed necessary to force the wind underneath the wings. Near the end of the track, when the propellers had generated enough speed, Orville felt himself get launched into the air. This was it. This was the moment of truth. Would he fly or would he fall?

The propellers pushed him forward and Orville just kept going up, and up, and up. He didn't go crashing to the ground. Over the sound of the motors, he could hear the cheers of the men below. This wasn't like gliding; Orville had done that plenty of times. This was flying. The motor turned the propellers which pushed him further and further forward, and Orville could make the plane turn by sliding to one side or the other and turning the wings and the tail. He was in full control of the plane, and he loved every minute of it.

For twelve glorious and magical seconds, Orville was like a bird in the sky. After he had landed, and everyone had come running over to congratulate him, he and Wilbur looked at each other without saying a word. They had achieved what they had set out to accomplish: not only had they proved that powered human flight was possible- they had made it a reality. Without wasting a lot of time celebrating, the men got busy in moving the plane back to the tracks to do the whole thing all over again. Twelve seconds was good, but they could do better. They had to do better. The Wright brothers would not settle for anything less than perfect.

Wow! Can you imagine what it would have been like to have been present during the first powered flight by the Wright brothers on that beach in Kitty Hawk, North Carolina? Can you imagine cheering Orville on as he soared into the clouds and turned and made his plane climb and turn as a bird? The picture above was snapped just as Orville took off at the beginning of that flight, and has become one of the most celebrated pictures ever taken. While the plane used by the Wright brothers looked a little different than the planes we see today, the Wright brothers made some significant discoveries that we still benefit from over a hundred years later!

Most of us have had the opportunity to ride in a plane. Sometimes they are small planes, just large enough for one or two people, and others are large enough to hold over eight hundred people! But one hundred years ago, in the year 1900, flight was still an uncommon thing. No one flew airplanes, and people only sometimes saw hot air balloons. Even those popular hot air balloons were slow and expensive to use. Some people had made gliders, but they could only stay in the air for short distances. The whole world had flying fever, but no one could figure out how to make it work- no one, that is, until the Wright brothers came along.

Have you ever heard of the Wright brothers? Did you know how important they were to the history of manned flight in the world? With their hard work, they were able to do what no else had ever done before them- they were able to send men into the air to fly like birds.

In this handbook, we will be looking a little more closely at what their hard work was all about and why they were so motivated. It will be a fascinating story of the power of a good imagination and what you can accomplish by working hard. What can you expect to learn as you read?

First, we will learn what led up to the first historic flight that we read about in the introduction, on December 17, 1903. For example, did you know that other famous inventors and engineers had been trying for a long time to get men into the air? What had they been able to accomplish, but what were some of the major problems that they were still having? Also, who were Orville and Wilbur Wright, and how did they get so interested in flight? Would you be surprised to find out that the famous inventors of the airplane got their start building printing presses and bicycles? We will learn more about their early history in this section.

In the following section, we will learn about mankind's long obsession with flight, and what were some of the scientific discoveries that allowed the Wright brothers to get their first plane into the air. We will also learn *why* so many people wanted to be like the birds and fly.

The next section will let us go along, step by step, with Orville and Wilbur as they design, test, modify, and retest their airplane designs. They used their heads to accomplish what had never before been done, although it wasn't always easy. Sometimes their planes flew as they were designed to, and sometimes they crashed into the ground. The men designed new tools and methods that are still used today to design and build airplanes. We will get to fly along with them on every test and feel the butterflies in our stomachs as the planes rise and fall in the sky.

The next section will talk about what it was like to be a kid during those days, the excitement that you would have felt and the way that your imagination would have run away from you. Then, we will see how the famous first flights ended, and what some of the immediate effects were on the lives of the Wright brothers.

Afterwards, we will see how the world was changed by the invention of the airplane. Initially the world didn't believe that the brothers had found a way to fly, and then everybody just went crazy and wanted to be a part of it. Entire governments soon got on board and wanted to see how they could use the plane to make their country stronger. We will also learn in this section about what happened to Orville and Wilbur after they became famous from inventing the airplane.

Planes have been flying ever since you were born, so why should you care about how they were invented? Why should you care about what happened over 100 years ago? Well, although humans have figured out a lot about flying, there is still a lot that we haven't been able to do yet, and we need smart people who can solve these problems for us. Will you be one of them? The story of the Wright brothers also shows us how beneficial it is to use your imagination, even when you are an adult, when you work at your job. Without imagination, things would hardly ever change. We need people with imagination even today.

We will also see how vital it is not to give up, even though the first results of something may not come out exactly how you would have liked. The Wright brothers gave us the first powered airplane, but they gave us a lot more: they gave us a splendid example of American ingenuity and imagination at work.

Let's learn more about the exciting adventures of these two brothers.

Chapter 1: What Led Up To the Invention of Flight?

The Wright brothers made the news and became an indispensable part of history when they made that historic flight back in 1903, but they sure weren't the only ones working on trying to make planes fly at that time- not by a long shot. People all around the world were working hard and learning from each other, each one trying to make a contribution to the overall effort. So while Orville and Wilbur Wright were the first ones to make it all come together and work, they owe a lot to the men that came before them and who made inventions and discoveries that Wrights later used. Who were some of the other people trying to learn how to fly? Let's find out.

George Cayley was a, English engineer who, back in the early to mid- eighteen hundreds, was able to make some fundamental discoveries about flight. He discovered that there were four powerful forces that affected any sort of flying vehicle: weight, lift, drag, and thrust. He was also able to (using his research) design the first glider that could carry a human. Do you know the difference between a glider and a powered airplane? A glider has no motor and relies on wind and air currents to sort of fall slowly to the ground (although experienced pilots can keep a glider in the air for a long time if they know how to take advantage of rising currents of warm air).

George Cayley, although he died in 1857, long before the Wright brothers were able to fly, made an important contribution to the history of flight, and the Wright brothers mentioned him by name later on after they had been successful.

Otto Lilienthal was a Prussia-born engineer who was interested in flying. Like George Cayley, he was also interested in learning how to fly using gliders. However, he made much more progress than Cayley ever could have dreamed of. After building a hill near Berlin, he designed and tested many different types of wing designs. He focused on using fixed wings and would attach the wings to himself, shifting his body weight to balance the glider.

Otto Lilienthal tested out his designs himself, as you can see in this picture from 1895.[2]

After he died a little later in a flying accident, Wilbur Wright wrote of him: "Of all the men who attacked the flying problem in the 19th century, Otto Lilienthal was easily the most important. ... It is true that attempts at gliding had been made hundreds of years before him, and that in the nineteenth century, Cayley, Spencer, Wenham, Mouillard, and many others were reported to have made feeble attempts to glide, but their failures were so complete that nothing of value resulted.[3]"

The Wright brothers learned a lot from the successes and failures of Otto Lilienthal, in particular, they tried to imitate the good parts of his wing design.

Samuel Langley was an American inventor who also wanted to fly, but who focused his energy con powered flight. Although his large-scale versions didn't have much success, his smaller models (using steam engines) proved that powered flight was not only possible but that it was the next logical step in flying. The Wright brothers ended up using an engine on their airplane also, although it was an internal combustion (gasoline) powered engine that turned the propellers, and not a steam engine.

---

[2] Image source: http://en.wikipedia.org/wiki/File:Otto_Lilienthal_gliding_experiment_ppmsca.02546.jpg

[3] Quotation source: http://en.wikipedia.org/wiki/Otto_Lilienthal

One of Samuel Langley's model airplanes flew ¾ mile using a small steam engine before crashing.[4]

These three men, along with others, had already done much to make flying a reality. Large gliders could carry men for long distances, and small models could be powered by engines and flown for thousands of feet, although larger versions with pilots crashed every time. What were the main problems faced by the world of aviation (flying) when the Wright brothers decided to get involved?

The idea of having fixed wings had been successful, but they didn't give the pilot much control over which way the plane went. Most early planes just flew in straight lines before landing (or crashing). So some method of steering the plane would have to be invented. Then, it was difficult to balance the weight especially with a large engine on board. And finally, the size of the propellers had proved to be a problem for many designers who like to use wide propellers (like the sails of a windmill). How would these large problems get solved? The Wright brothers were the ones who were able to look at all of the problems facing early aviators and to say: "Yeah, we can figure that out." But how did these two brothers, raised in Ohio as part of a large family, ever get involved in building airplanes? Let's find out.

Wilbur Wright was born on April 16, 1867, and his brother Orville born on August 19, 1871. Always very close as they grew up, the Wright family was a family that valued imagination and hard work. Their parents always encouraged the boys to explore, to ask questions, and to read all the books that they could get their hands on. As a family, they would get together and debate topics, learning how to think clearly and logically and to try to win others over to their position.

Wilbur did well in school and was on his way to college when he got hurt pretty badly during a hockey game. He got pretty depressed and decided to stay and home and work with his brother and best friend, Orville. Orville had never liked school and preferred to work with his hands. He dropped out his junior year and designed and built a printing press, which he and his brother used to open a print shop a couple of years later. The newspaper, called the *West Side News*, generated some money for the boys and allowed them to open a bike shop a few years later, in 1892.

The whole country was interested in buying and riding bicycles, so the brothers originally opened a shop with the intention of selling other people's bikes, but soon they were selling bikes that they had designed and built themselves. They loved every minute of the process of drawing out a plan, building a test model, and then seeing the final results being sold and used in the streets.

Meanwhile, both brothers had a deep love of science and were interested in reading different magazines and books on the subject. They corresponded with different scientists and were able to keep up to speed on the different discoveries and inventions that were being made around the world. As the most influential minds of the day were busy talking about flying, it was not long before the Wrights themselves became interested in the subject. In fact, since their father gave them a small paper helicopter as children, they had been curious about flight.

As adults, it wasn't long before they decided that they would like to give powered flight a try themselves. In 1899, the brothers started developing their first attempt at an airplane.

The problems we saw earlier would all have to be solved in man was ever to fly, and the Wright brothers were going to do their best to solve those problems. But you might be asking yourself: why was everybody so worked up about flying in the first place? What did they ever hope to accomplish by building planes and going all over the place?

Chapter 2: Why Did the Invention of Flight Happen?

Humans have always wanted to make the impossible a reality. For centuries, men looked up at the birds flying high in the sky and asked themselves: why can't I do that? Over two thousand years ago, there was even a Greek story about a young man named Icarus who put on two wings built by his father Daedalus and then used them to fly away from the island of Crete, only to crash into the sea when the sun melted the wax holding the feathers to the wings. Even though the story was not true, it shows that even way back then humans were thinking of ways of getting into the sky.

In the year 559, one young Chinese prince named Yuan Huangtou was forced to be the test pilot of a large kite designed to carry a man. Even though the tyrant who made him be a test pilot expected him to fall and die, the kite ended up taking him over one and a half miles away from his prison, and he survived the flight. Everyone was impressed that something had been built that could carry a man through the air for such a long distance.

Not a lot more happened during the next few hundred years in the world of flight, but in about 1010, the first glider was built by an English monk named Eilmer of Malmesbury. He wrote that he flew 200 yards before falling and breaking both his legs. According to him, he would have flown further if he had given his glider a tail, but out of concern for his safety, he was told to stop experimenting. As a result, his improved glider was never built.

On November 21, 1783, French aviator Pilâtre de Rozier made the first manned hot air balloon flight. Taking off from in front of the French king, Louis XVI, he and a companion named the Marquis d'Arlandes flew up to a height of about 3,000 feet. The flight lasted for twenty-five minutes and took them a distance of about five and a half miles. A small iron stove burned the fuel that heated the air and made the balloon rise. Everyone was genuinely excited by this new technology, and the race became to see who could make their balloons go further and higher.

On July 15, 1784, the Robert brothers flew for forty five minutes in France with a new type of hot air balloon that could be steered instead of simply relying on the air currents and wind. This new balloon, called a dirigible, used a rudder (like on a boat) to sail through the air as if it were a giant sea.

Henri Giffard was a French engineer who made a significant contribution to flight: he added an engine to power the steerable hot air balloons. In 1852, he flew 17 miles in a steam-powered airship.

Henry Giffard's powered hot air balloon flying over Paris in 1878.[5]

The world's scientists and engineers were getting closer and closer to making powered flight a reality. The focus had been for a long time on large balloons and rigid dirigibles, but as humans learned more about the atmosphere and physics, it was clear that the time was coming when powered glider would

[5]   Image   source:
http://en.wikipedia.org/wiki/File:Captive_balloon_of_Henri_Giffard
_over_Paris_1878.jpg

become a reality. Engines were being made smaller and more powerful, and there was an ever larger interest in flying.

After seeing how hard humans have worked during hundreds of years to fly, do you ever ask yourself why everyone was so crazy to fly? Well, think about what flying meant to people living one hundred years ago. Flying would mean travelling long distances in shorter times. It would mean having an advantage over the enemy in war, and it would mean growing in our knowledge and abilities as a species. Humans have always had astounding imaginations, and they have always made the impossible a reality. Flight seemed like a dream for a long time, but the hard work of so many dedicated men and women were sure to make it happen eventually.

By the time the Wright brothers got involved in the race to become the first to make powered flight happen, people had been using hot air balloons for over one hundred years and powered balloons for almost fifty. But no one had been able to make the smaller crafts, the ones that looked more like birds, fly under their own power. They could only glide for a short distance before crashing. How did the Wright brothers solve the problems that no one else had been able to solve? Let's find out.

Chapter 3: What Happened During the Wright Brother's Contribution To the Invention of Flight?

In 1899, after having become successful bicycle designers and salesman, the Wright brothers decided to begin working on powered flight. The first step was to design a model that they could test and look for ways to improve. The fixed wing glider had been the primary design used by inventors for a long time. The wings were "fixed" which meant that they could not be moved or adjusted. But sometimes, in the case of a strong gust of wind or with problems balancing the weight, this fixed-wing design led to disaster. What could the solution be?

The brothers decided to look more closely at flight in nature, specifically at pigeons. Pigeons, because they had been flying well for a long time, seemed to know what they were doing. This idea of trying copy nature is called biomimetics and is still used by scientists today. What did Wilbur and Orville Wright discover when they studied how pigeons fly? They discovered that the pigeon makes lots of tiny adjustments with its wings in order to turn and control its flight. To turn left, it will tilt its left wing up and its right wing down. To turn right, it does the opposite. To go up or down, it tilts both wings up or down together. Using the four fundamental forces described by George Cayley back in the early to mid- eighteen hundreds (weight, lift, drag, and thrust) the pigeons were able to fly exactly where they wanted to.

The Wright brothers realized that the first essential thing that they should include in their design should be a way to make the wings flexible. While taking an inner tube out of a cardboard box one day, Wilbur noticed that he could twist the ends of long box in opposite directions and make it look just like the wing of a pigeon. He realized that this was the type of wing that they would have to design.

The first glider built by the brothers wasn't actually made for a pilot (it was still too dangerous) but was built to be flown like a kite and controlled by pulling on ropes. They wanted to see how the flexible wing design (called "wing warp" worked using real winds). The brothers needed a place with strong, steady winds and lots of open space where they could work in peace. They wrote to the United States National Weather Bureau and were told that Kitty Hawk, North Carolina, would be the perfect place. So in the fall of 1900 they went there with their model glider to test out the flexible wings and to see how they could make it better. The glider weighed fifty pounds and had a seventeen-foot wingspan. Although Wilbur climbed aboard for a few tests (while the glider was held in place by ropes), mostly they used sandbags to give the glider balance and to simulate the weight of a pilot.

You can see the Wright Brother's 1900 glider being flown without a pilot in Kitty Hawk.[6]

The tests showed that the model was good, but they decided to build a bigger one which could safely hold a pilot and that would have landing gear and better controls.

After going back to Ohio to work on their design, the brothers returned to Kitty Hawk in the summer of 1901 to test out the new design. This glider was even bigger: it weighed 100 pounds and had a twenty-two

[6]   Image   source:
http://en.wikipedia.org/wiki/File:WrightBrothers1900Glider.jpg

foot wingspan. The brothers had also added boards on the bottom of the glider to make the landing smoother. During their test flights on the first day, Wilbur flew 17 glides. During the best one, he was in the air for twenty seconds and covered almost four hundred feet. The control system worked and let him turn just like a pigeon does in the air. His seat was connected to some wires, and by sliding his seat to the right or to the left, he could make the glider turn the way he wanted it. A forward elevator (a special wing placed on the front of the plane) allowed the pilot to control the up and down angle of the plane.

This picture shows Wilbur Wright in 1901 just after landing. The forward elevator is in front of his head.[7]

[7]   Image   source: http://en.wikipedia.org/wiki/File:Wright_1901_glider_landing.jpg

The flights showed that the new wing warp design was successful, but the brothers also saw some serious problems. For example, the wing warp design, which allowed them to control the glider, sometimes made it spin out of control. The forward elevators that made the plane tilt up or down (and go higher or lower) needed to be improved, and the wings didn't have enough lifting power to make the plane fly high enough or far enough.

At this moment, after so much planning, and after so much hard work and money invested in the project, the brothers felt pretty disappointed and were worried that man would not get to fly anytime soon. But, Wilbur and Orville Wright didn't give up. They wanted to keep trying to find solutions and keep working hard. So the Wright brothers went back to Ohio to work on a better design. During the winter of 1901, they invented a brilliant mechanism to test out new plane wing designs: a wind tunnel.

This six-foot long wind tunnel allowed the Wright brothers to design wings that would work better.[8]

By testing out different types of wings, the brothers were able to see which types of wings (how thick, how long, how wide) worked the best to get lift. Lift is where the wind goes under a wing and pushes it up into the sky. Much cheaper than building lots of gliders, the wind tunnel provided a steady wind of 27 miles per hour and allowed Wilbur and Orville to design the best type of wings possible. In fact, scientists today still know how important wind tunnels are when designing airplanes and cars, and they still use them.

In 1902, the brothers went back to Kitty Hawk to test out the new and improved glider wings. The new glider had a thirty-two foot wingspan and a tail to

[8]   Image   source:
http://www.newworldencyclopedia.org/entry/File:WB_Wind_Tunn
el.jpg

help stabilize it (it would fix the problem with the forward elevators). The larger wings would keep the plane from spinning out of control and would give it greater lift, allowing it to go higher into the sky and to stay in the air longer. This glider was a whopping success for the Wright brothers and could fly for distances of up to 500 feet!

This third design showed that the brothers were on the right track. The glider was easier to control, was more stable when in the air, and could fly for longer distances. Now, the most critical phase of the project had come: adding a motor to power the aircraft so that it could fly anywhere, not only on windy beaches. Up until this point, other inventors had tried to add motors to their planes, and some were successful when working with smaller models. However, no one had been able to build a large airplane that could be powered by a motor and piloted by a man. The Wright brothers had notable success building gliders, but could they build the first powered airplane? They were sure going to try their best.

After going back to Ohio to work on designing propellers and to find a small engine to put onboard their plane, the brothers returned to Kitty Hawk in the fall of 1903 to get some more practice with their glider and to put together their new plane. Called "The Flyer", this plane weighed over 700 pounds. The tail on this plane was moveable, and moved together with the wings to help make sharper and more controlled turns. A motor was mounted to the right of the pilot and used rubber belts to turn the propellers. The propellers themselves were an invention of the Wrights also. Unlike other inventors, who tried to use wide propeller blades, the brothers saw that thin blades moved faster and were more effective at generating forward motion.

On the beach, the brothers laid out a long wooden track that would help the plane to go forward and to gain enough speed to generate lift and to take off into the air. Wilbur took the first try on December 15. Orville ran with him down the track as the plan gained speed, and thirty five feet the plane took off and went up into the air. But after only three and a half seconds the plane crashed down hard into the ground. Wilbur was okay, but the plane had received some damage. It would take about two days to fix the plane and to get it ready to fly again.

On December 17, 1903, the Wright brothers took their repaired plane out for another try. This time, as we saw in the introduction, it was Orville who would be the pilot. With Wilbur running alongside the plane as it went down the track, Orville kept the plane steady as it went faster and faster. Then, after about 35 feet, the plane lifted off the ground and one of the men who were helping the brothers took a picture, the picture that you saw at the beginning of the handbook. The plane took off into the air, and this time it did not crash. For twelve incredible seconds, the propellers pushed the heavy plane through the air, and under its own power the plane flew up and up and turned under Orville's control.

During three more flights that day, the brothers were eventually able to get the plane to stay in the air for more time and for a longer distance. During the last flight, when Wilbur was the pilot, The Flyer stayed in the air for 59 seconds and travelled 852 feet!

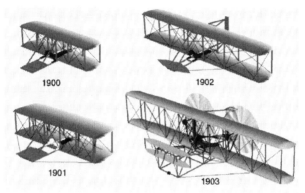

These are the four gliders/airplanes built by the Wright brothers during their flight tests.[9]

The Wright brothers had managed to do what no other human had been able to accomplish: they had been able to build an airplane that, powered by an engine, flew and turned as a pilot controlled its every move. A new era of human technology had begun, the age of human flight; and the world had the Wright brothers to thank for making it all happen!

---

[9] Image source: http://www.space.com/16596-wright-flyer-first-airplane.html

Chapter 4: What Was It Like To Be a Kid Back Then?

Being a kid back then would have been exciting because you would have seen history being made! For the longest time, humans had looked up at the sky and wished that they could move through the air like the birds. But for centuries it seemed like the technology would never exist and that man would be forever doomed to walk on the earth like the animals. But little by little, as a kid living back then, you would have seen men across the world trying to beat gravity.

Kids love to do crazy stuff, and maybe you have even jumped from a tree house with a blanket for a parachute or bounced up and down for hours on a trampoline. Kids love to feel butterflies in their stomachs as they fall or slide or roll around. Can you imagine what it would have felt like to fly on a glider high in the air for long distances? You would have felt like a superhero! Imagine being down on the beach and watching the Wright brothers testing out their airplane. You would have seen how they believed so much in their work that they risked their own lives by climbing into the plane and trying to make it fly.

When the plane crashed, would you have been sad to see that it didn't work? Would you have expected the brothers to just give up and go home to do what they were already good at: making bicycles? Some people may have expected that, but how would you have felt watching the brothers get up from the ground, dust themselves off, and get right back on that plane to try it again? Would you have felt inspired?

Watching Orville and Wilbur Wright would have taught you a valuable lesson: don't give up even though something looks difficult. Don't stop trying to make your idea into a success just because you have a failure or a setback. Some of the greatest people in the world, including the Wright brothers, needed more than one try to get it right.

As you watched that first successful flight on December 17, 1903, surely your mind would have been full of possibilities. You would have imagined all that humans would be capable of now that they could fly. You could imagine them going from one country to another, over mountains and oceans, in short amounts of time. You could imagine seeing the world from high up, like birds do. And if you had an exceptionally good imagination, you would probably start to wonder how high up humans could go, and if they could ever get as high up as the moon and the planets beyond.

The new era of human flight was going to be a time when the world changed, and when the new technology would be used by governments, large companies, and independent pilots everywhere. It would be a time when mankind would take a giant leap forward and realize that nothing was impossible as long as they kept pushing forward and trying to solve some of the greatest problems.

It would have been exciting to be a kid back then and witness history.

Chapter 5: How Did the Wright Brothers' Contribution To the Invention of Flight End?

The Wright brothers had witnesses and photographic evidence to prove that they were the first ones to successfully fly a powered airplane. Although they wished to keep their achievement quiet for a while, a telegraph operator leaked out the news, and the next day newspapers everywhere had different versions of the story. Although some of them weren't accurate at all, the world was put on notice that humans had figured out a way to fly.

The news travelled quickly around the world, but some people refused to believe that such a thing was possible. They thought that surely this was some sort of a joke or even a lie. Such people refused to believe that anyone could fly until they saw it with their own eyes. Unfortunately, The Flyer used by the Wrights on that famous December day was flipped over by some strong winds and was damaged so badly that it would never fly again. But now that they had a working design, the brothers knew that they would soon be in the air again.

Avoiding the press for some time, the brothers decided to build better and better machines. By October 5, 1905, the brothers had mastered flight. Orville made a 38 minute flight that took him a distance of 24.5 miles. The flight only ended because he had run out of fuel, but he was still able to land the plane safely. Convinced that the plane was ready to show the world, the brothers decided to put all of their hopes on selling copies of their planes to interested persons and to start a company. The sold their bicycle business and put all their time and efforts into designing and flying airplanes.

To silence the doubters (who because of the lack of international press and photographs didn't believe the brothers' claims) and to show off their inventions, the Wright brothers began to travel from one place to another demonstrating how their airplane flied. But to make sure that no one could steal their ideas, the brothers would fly their planes (which now had two seats for the pilot and a passenger) only if the person had signed a contract showing interest in buying the planes.

In the United States, the government had been disappointed with the results of their investments in flight. The Langley Aerodrome cost a lot of money to make, but during its two test flights in front of prominent officials and reporters the plane crashed down into the Potomac River and never actually flew.

Because they couldn't expect anything from the U.S. government, the brothers went to France, the country that had been the home of so many famous aviators and engineers throughout history.

In France, lots of people were just as skeptical, but they gave the brothers an opportunity to prove them wrong. On August 8, 1908, Wilbur flew in front of an amazed French audience that was shocked as he made controlled turns and even flew in a complete circle. Even though that flight lasted less than two minutes, it was clear that the Wright brothers had built a machine capable to doing brand new things. During the new few days, Wilbur continued his demonstrations, even flying figure eights in the sky, impressing everybody who saw him.

After several months of impressing people all over France (including the kings of Spain, England, and Italy), the Wright brothers returned home as heroes. Together with their sister Katherine, they were the three most influential people in the whole world at that time. In July of 1909, they demonstrated their airplane for the United States Army and were able to both fly faster than 40 miles per hour and to make a safe landing. The government bought the airplane for $35,000 (equal to about $800,000 today).

The experiments had been successful, and now the brothers were business partners and world famous inventors. Although they never flew together to avoid any tragedies, on May 25, 1910, Orville and Wilbur Wright made a special exception and took their first and only flight together. Then Orville took up their 82 year-old father for his first and only flight. As the plane climbed up to 350 feet above the ground, the brother's father Milton Wright yelled out "Higher, Orville, higher!"

The Wright brothers had solved the problems that no one else had been able to do, and they had been able to repeat time and time again the wondrous flights that made them famous. People all over the world were excited to see what would happen in this new era of flight.

Chapter 6: What Happened After the Wright Brothers' Contribution To the Invention of Flight?

After selling their airplane to the United States army, the Wright brothers spent some time teaching army officers how to fly it. It wasn't long before the first Wright brothers' plane was outfitted with a machine gun for military use.

The brothers themselves got to see one of their planes, the Vin Fiz, make a cross country trip all the way to California. Over a period of 84 days, the airplane made 70 short trips, where people from the local towns would come out and have a look at the amazing plane.

In 1914, the Aviation Section of the Signal Corps (part of the U.S. Army) was created, using primarily planes made by the Wright Brothers. The planes had become a part of the war machine, and in future years planes would decide entire battle (like the Battle of Midway during World War Two).

The Wright brothers themselves were pleased to see that the world liked their planes. Although they had to fight to get patents that would protect all of their hard work, they were able to stay busy and productive running their new company, the Wright Company, established by them on November 22, 1909. Wilbur, who was better with business things, was the President of the company, while Orville, who was better inventing and designing, was the Vice President. The brothers always shared credit for everything they did, and were a formidable team.

The Wright brothers in 1910.[10]

10   Image   source:

But all that changed in 1912.

Wilbur Wright got sick while on a business trip in Boston in April of 1912. He was diagnosed with Typhoid fever and died just a few weeks later on May 30, 1912. He had never married, deciding to focus all of his energy on making and testing airplanes. His brother Orville, who had been his partner and best friend for most of his life, was devastated. He sold the business in 1915 and decided to focus for the rest of his life on helping others to fly and develop new technologies. He even worked with the National Advisory Committee for Aeronautics (NACA), an agency that was the first version of what would later be called the National Aeronautics and Space Administration (NASA). Orville himself died on January 30, 1948 of a heart attack.

The Wright brothers were raised when everyone used horses and buggies to travel. But by the time Orville died, there were fast cars on the streets and rocket planes flying nearly 1,000 miles per hour. Thanks to his and Wilbur's contributions to the invention of flight, the world had changed, and it would never be the same.

http://en.wikipedia.org/wiki/File:Wright_Brothers_in_1910.jpg

Conclusion

Orville and Wilbur Wright were two extraordinary men. Although they had been born to a quiet family, their thirst for knowledge, their imaginations, and their willingness to work hard helped them to do what no one else had been able to. They were able to fly like birds in the sky. Did you learn something new from this handbook? Let's review what we saw.

First, we learned what led up to the first historic flight that we read about in the introduction, on December 17, 1903. For example, do you remember the other famous inventors and engineers that had been trying for a long time to get men into the air? We saw that some men were able to use kites, gliders, and even hot air balloons to get people closer to flying. While all those technologies were entertaining, none of them let us fly like birds. They were generally short flights that moved slowly and were difficult to control. While those inventors had been able to accomplish a lot, they still had some serious problems, like making turns, designing the propellers, and keeping the plane in the air for longer periods of times.

We also learned more about who Orville and Wilbur Wright were and how got so interested in flight. We learned that they were two bright boys who were encouraged to learn as much as they could about the world around them. Were you surprised to find out that the famous inventors of the airplane got their start building printing presses and bicycles? But because of their hard work and their imagination, they were able to accomplish a lot.

In the following section, we learned about mankind's long obsession with flight, and what some of the scientific discoveries were which allowed the Wright brothers to get their first plane into the air. We saw how learning more about lift, drag, and even the makeup of the atmosphere made it easier to design airplane wings and propellers. We also learned *why* so many people wanted to be like the birds and fly. Do you remember how a lot of people wanted to use airplanes for travel and for fighting their wars?

The next section let us go along, step by step, with Orville and Wilbur as they design, test, modify, and retest their airplane designs. We watched as they used their heads to accomplish what had never before been done, although it wasn't always easy. Sometimes their planes flew as they were designed to, and sometimes they crashed into the ground. The men designed new tools and methods that are still used today to design and build airplanes. We got to fly along with them on every test and felt the butterflies in our stomachs as the planes rise and fall in the sky. The brothers learned something from each failure, and each test was better than the last one.

The next section talked about what it was like to be a kid during those days, the excitement that you would have felt and the way that your imagination would have run away from you. Then, we saw how the famous first flights ended, and what some of the immediate effects were on the lives of the Wright brothers. We saw how they travelled the world showing everyone their new planes, and how everyone just went crazy when they saw how cool flying could be. We also saw how the Wright brothers became super famous almost overnight.

After that, we saw how the world was changed by the invention of the airplane. Initially the world didn't believe that the brothers had found a way to fly, and then everybody just went crazy and wanted to be a part of it. Entire governments soon got on board and wanted to see how they could use the plane to make their country stronger. We watched as they sold their first plane and as they had to fight to get patents to protect it. We also learned in this section about what happened to Orville and Wilbur after they got famous from inventing the airplane. We saw how they built a first-rate company that kept building and testing new types of planes. Finally, we learned how they died, and in the case of Orville, how much the world had changed.

What is the most important lesson that you have learned from this handbook? The success of the Wright brothers was not due to luck or to being in the right place at the right time. They were the first ones to fly because they learned from everyone else who had come before them and were willing to take risks. When their experiments failed or didn't work out just right, they learned from the mistakes and tried again. They used their imaginations and worked hard.

What about you? Do you have a good imagination? When you look at problems, instead of feeling sad about them or overwhelmed, can you try to think of creative ways of solving them to help others? Where would we be if it weren't for the hard work of the Wright brothers? We would still be driving around on the ground, and it would take forever to get where we're going. The world would seem like a much bigger place.

Learn a lesson from Orville and Wilbur: use your imagination, work hard, and learn from your mistakes. If you do, the sky will be the limit!

49001955R00026

Made in the USA
Columbia, SC
15 January 2019